ZLATA'S DIARY

by
Zlata Filipović

Teacher Guide

Written by
Stacie Lee Champlin Dreibrodt

Note

The Penguin paperback edition of this book published by Penguin Books Ltd, ©1994, was used to prepare this guide. Page references may differ in other editions.

Please note: This novel deals with the issue of war. Please assess the appropriateness of this book for the age level and maturity of your students prior to reading and discussing it with your class.

ISBN 1-58130-704-7

To order, contact your local school supply store, or—

Novel Units, Inc.
P.O. Box 433
Bulverde, TX 78163-0433

Web site: www.educyberstor.com

Table of Contents

Skills and Strategies

Vocabulary
  Definition, application,
  vocabulary games

Listening/Speaking
  Class discussion,
  interviewing

Thinking
  Research, critical thinking,
  personal interpretation

Literary Elements
  Character analysis, literary
  analysis, metaphors

Comprehension
  Predictions, analysis,
  applications

Cross Curricular
  Drama, illustrations,
  mobile, music, math,
  geography

Writing
  Creative writing, diary
  entries, compare/contrast,
  letter, persuasive, play,
  speech

Summary

Zlata Filipović is a happy young girl who lives in Sarajevo. Her life is a good one filled with family and friends. However, when war breaks out in her hometown, her happy life is shattered. Through Zlata's entries into "Mimmy," her diary, we are able to learn of the atrocities through which she has lived. She describes times without food, water, and electricity. We are given an in-depth look at war through the eyes of a young student.

About the Author

Zlata Filipović was a resident of Sarajevo where she lived with her mother and father. She celebrates her eleventh birthday at the beginning of the diary and shortly after her thirteenth birthday, she and her family are allowed to leave for Paris. Zlata and her family now reside in Ireland. Her book has been published throughout the world.

Initiating Activities

1. Explain to the students that they will be reading the diary of a young girl from war-torn Sarajevo. Ask the students to keep a diary that describes the events of their lives. Encourage them to write in the diary in response to what they learn from Zlata.

2. Ask the students to consider what it would be like if their life was turned upside down. As a class, come up with some expectations that they have for hearing about life in wartime. Compare these expectations to the information given in the text.

3. Ask the students to write about the importance of each one of the following ideas:

   family   freedom   basic needs   fear   war

4. Many different countries and places are mentioned throughout the story. As a class, create a large map that can be displayed while studying the book. Locate all of the places mentioned on the map. This will help the students to visualize the locations.

5. Ask the students to respond to each of the following statements. Collect their comments and save them during the unit. Ask the students to respond to the statements again after reading the text. Return the original papers, and ask the students to explain any differences.
   - Children in other countries have different lives.
   - War always involves two active parties.
   - If there is no shooting, there is no war.
   - War is a necessary evil.
   - The main result of war is that it is dangerous to go out into the streets.
   - If you keep to yourself, you are basically unaffected by a war.
   - Everyone deserves a peaceful childhood.
   - Once you leave the war behind, you can go on with your regular life.
   - Money is the solution to difficulties during war.
   - Only those directly involved in battle are ever injured or killed during a war.

6. Ask students to fill in the Prediction Chart (pages 5-6 of this guide) as they read the book.

Vocabulary Activities

1. Definition Scramble: Write each vocabulary word on an index card. Write each definition on another index card. Pass these cards out as the students enter the classroom. Tell them to read the card and then to trade it. Ask them to do this two more times. Then have the students find their partner, the one with the definition to match the word or vice versa. Once they have paired off, ask them to stand at the front of the room. Ask them to recite their word and definition to the class.

2. Word Wall: Assign each student a vocabulary word. Ask them to teach that word to the class. Encourage them to come up with a creative way to help the class remember the definition. Place each word up on a bulletin board once it has been taught; leave it there for the remainder of the unit.

3. Vocabulary Bingo: Create bingo cards that have both words and definitions on them. Make sure all of the boards are different. Call out some words and definitions. If the students have the definition or the word to match what you read, then they can cover that space on their card. Play as you would a regular game of bingo.

4. Who am I?: Assign each student a word, and tell them to keep their word a secret. Allow students to ask each other "yes" or "no" questions in order to help them to determine the other students' words. For example, "Are you a verb?" or, "Do you describe something?" etc. Once the word has been identified, the person who identified it must be able to state the corresponding definition.

5. Round Robin: Make a list of vocabulary words. Have the students create a story by taking turns making up sentences, adding on to the story that has already been started. Each student should add at least one sentence using a vocabulary word. Keep going around the room until all the words are used.

Using Predictions in the Novel Unit Approach

We all make predictions as we read—little guesses about what will happen next, how a conflict will be resolved, which details will be important to the plot, which details will help fill in our sense of a character. Students should be encouraged to predict, to make sensible guesses as they read the novel.

As students work on their predictions, these discussion questions can be used to guide them: What are some of the ways to predict? What is the process of a sophisticated reader's thinking and predicting? What clues does an author give to help us make predictions? Why are some predictions more likely to be accurate than others?

Create a chart for recording predictions. This could be either an individual or class activity. As each subsequent chapter is discussed, students can review and correct their previous predictions about plot and characters as necessary.

Use the facts and ideas the author gives.

Use your own prior knowledge.

Apply any new information (i.e., from class discussion) that may cause you to change your mind.

Predictions:

5

Prediction Chart

What characters have we met so far?	What is the conflict in the story?	What are your predictions?	Why did you make those predictions?

Using Character Webs in the Novel Unit Approach

Attribute webs are simply a visual representation of a character from the novel. They provide a systematic way for students to organize and recap the information they have about a particular character. Attribute webs may be used after reading the novel to recapitulate information about a particular character, or completed gradually as information unfolds. They may be completed individually or as a group project.

One type of character attribute web uses these divisions:

- How a character acts and feels. (How does the character act? How do you think the character feels? How would you feel if this happened to you?)

- How a character looks. (Close your eyes and picture the character. Describe him/her to me.)

- Where a character lives. (Where and when does the character live?)

- How others feel about the character. (How does another specific character feel about our character?)

In group discussion about the characters described in student attribute webs, the teacher can ask for backup proof from the novel. Inferential thinking can be included in the discussion.

Attribute webs need not be confined to characters. They may also be used to organize information about a concept, object, or place.

Attribute Web

Directions: Create an attribute web for Zlata that gives information about her character. Cite specific passages and page numbers from the book to support your ideas.

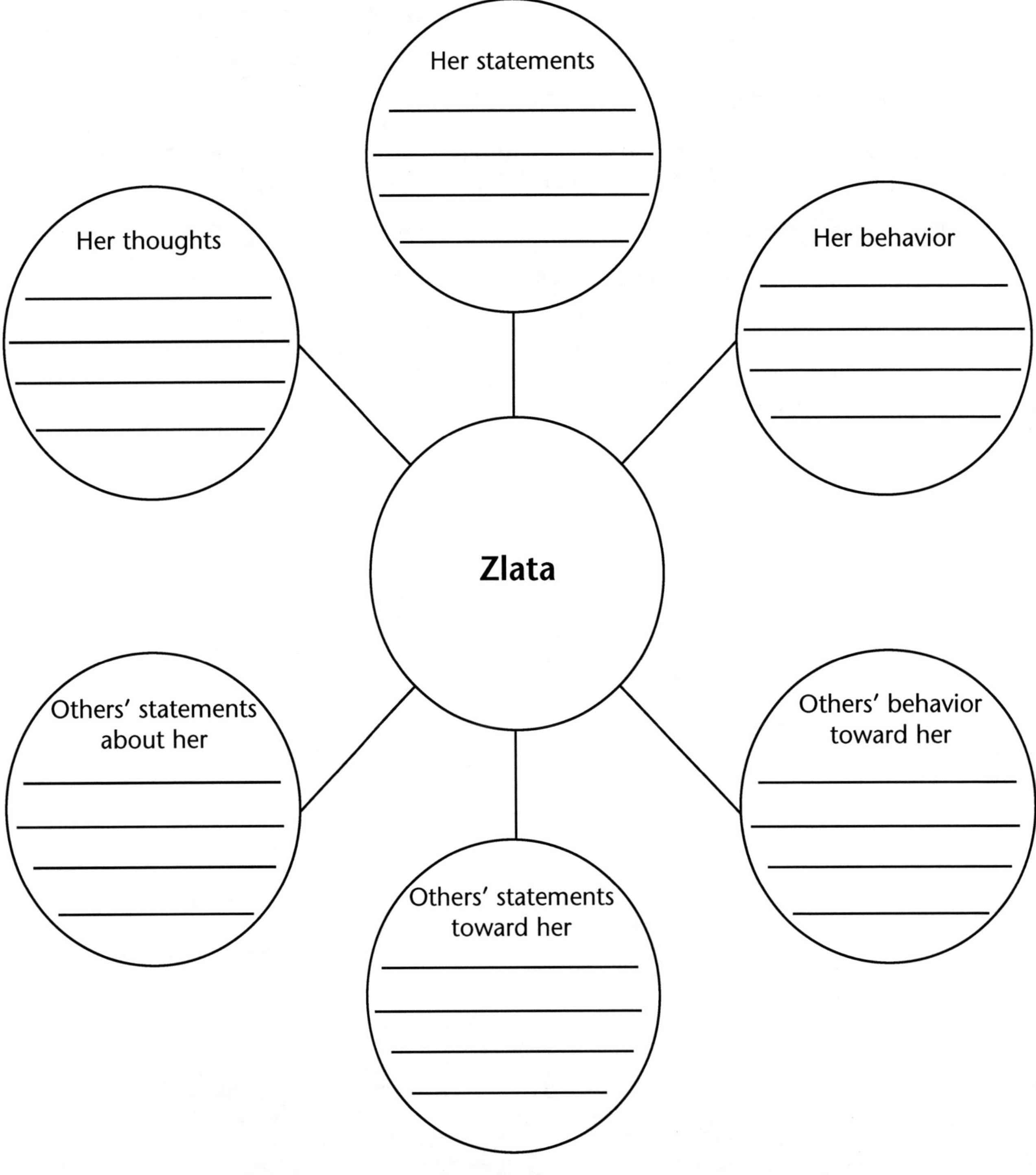

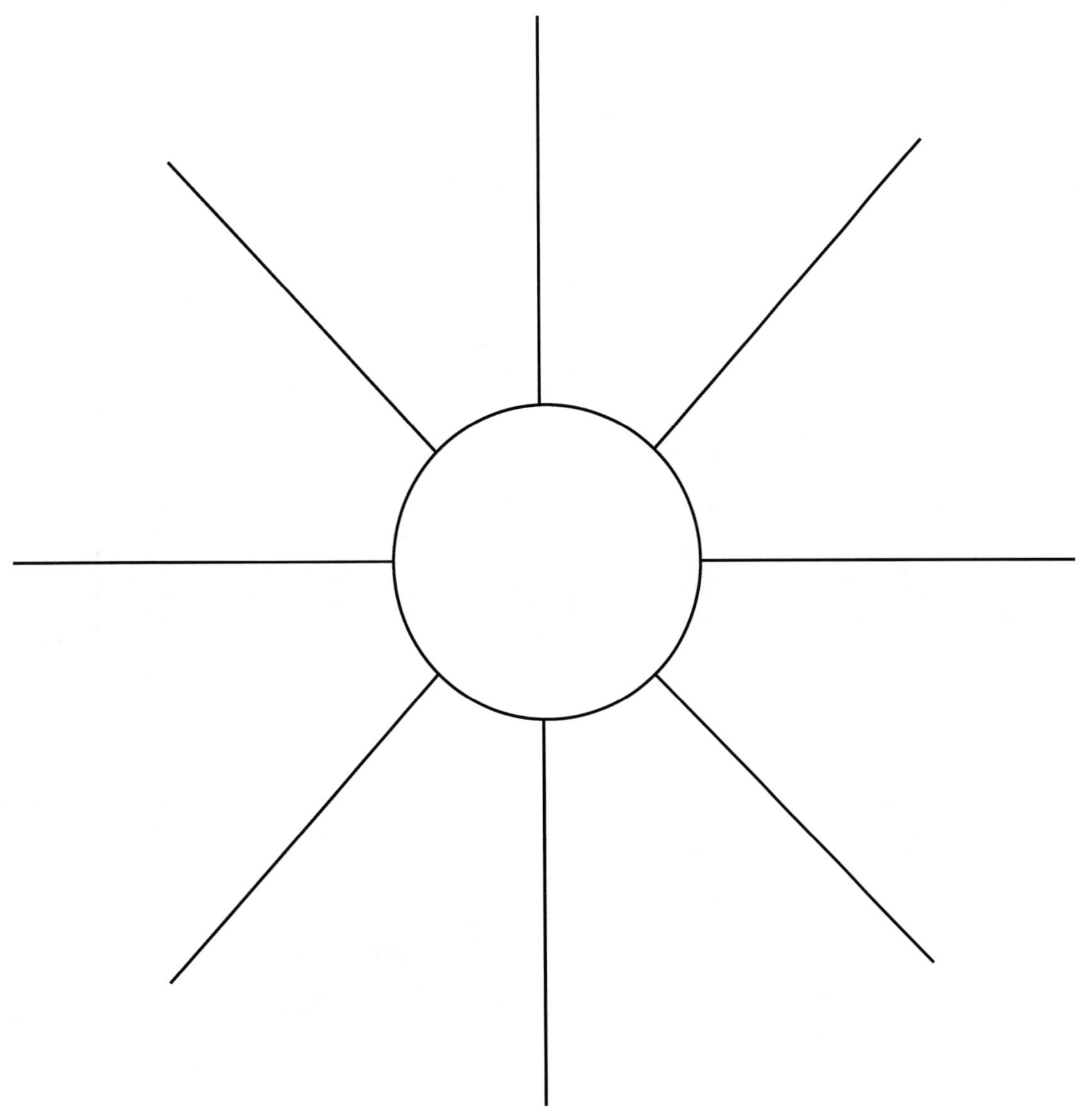

Story Map

Directions: Fill in each box below with information about the novel.

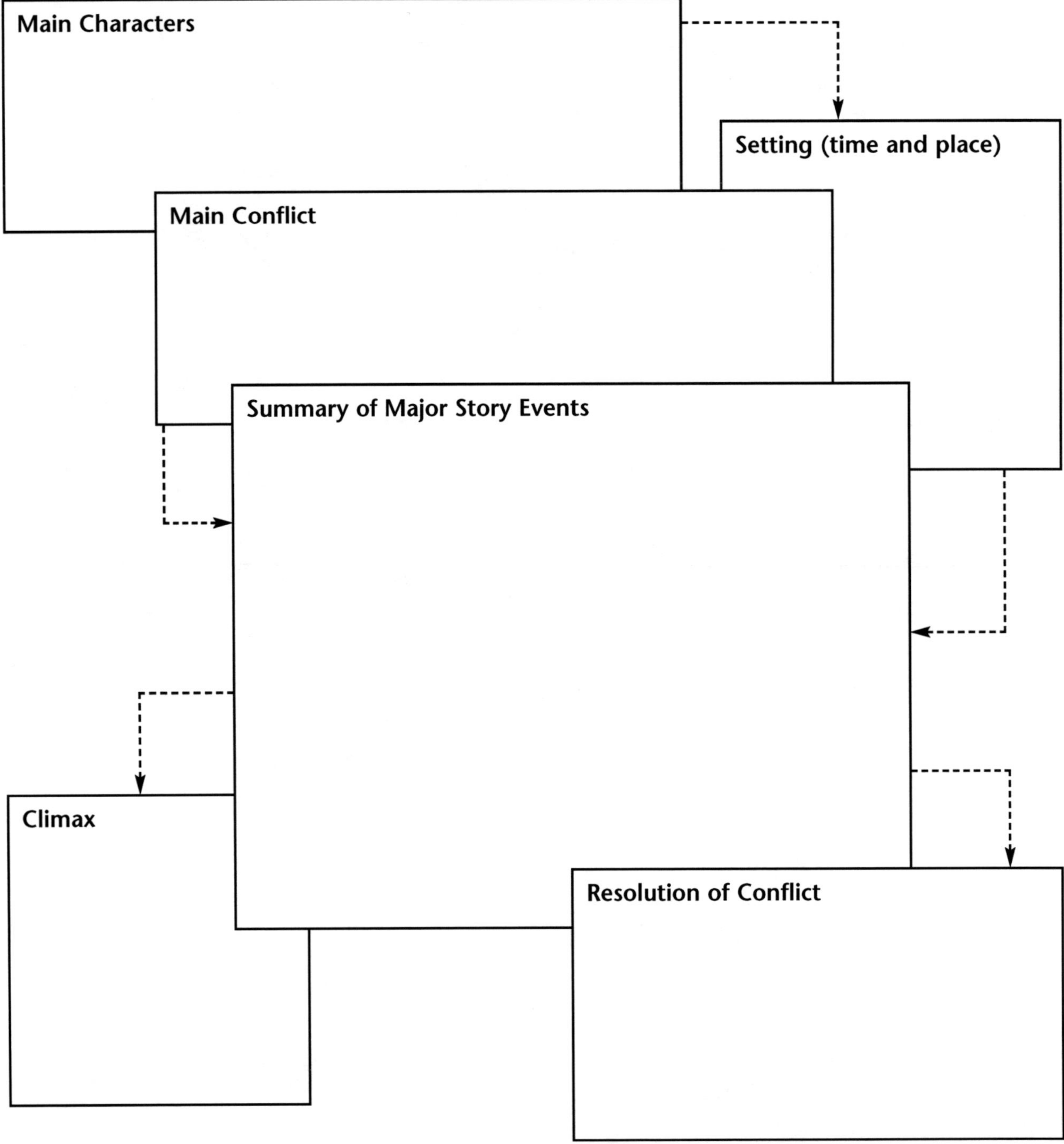

Vocabulary

barricades (*v*)	irrevocably (*v*)	artillery (*vi*)	shrapnel (*vi*)
cowering (*vii*)	humanitarian (*vii*)	diligent (*vii*)	resigned (*ix*)
stoical (*ix*)	notorious (*x*)	traumatized (*xii*)	solfeggio (1)
herbarium (4)	politics (6)	antibiotic (12)	pessimist (13)
inspiration (13)	persistent (14)	proverbial (17)	epidemic (23)

Discussion Questions

1. Why does Zlata write, "I'm all alone here" (page *vi*)? (*Most of her friends' families have chosen to flee Sarajevo.*)

2. Write a brief summary explaining the information conveyed in the introduction. (*Answers will vary.*)

3. What kind of person is Zlata? (*Answers will vary.*)

4. Why are we told of all of the tragedies in Dubrovnik? How does Zlata feel about the war in Dubrovnik? (*It is foreshadowing for what is to come in Sarajevo; she finds it horrible and impossible to imagine.*)

5. Study the pictures of Zlata. How are they different from family pictures you have? How are they the same? (*Answers will vary.*)

6. According to Zlata, how does the war in Dubrovnik affect people in Sarajevo? (*Answers will vary.*)

7. How is Zlata like you? How is she different? (*Answers will vary.*)

8. Describe Zlata's life. How do you think it is going to change? (*Answers will vary.*)

9. What would happen if you ever found yourself in Zlata's position? (*Answers will vary.*)

10. What could Zlata do to help prepare herself for the upcoming situation? (*Answers will vary.*)

11. What conclusions can you draw about Zlata? (*Answers will vary.*)

12. What conclusions can you draw about Zlata's parents? (*Answers will vary.*)

Supplementary Activities

1. Creative Writing: When Zlata plays the piano she is able to "escape" the atrocities of war. Have the students write a song or describe an activity that would help them to escape.

2. Music/Reading: Find a sample of music Zlata might have played at the piano during the war (see page 107 of the text for suggestions). Play it in the background while students take turns reading sections of the diary aloud.

3. Research: Have the students research the following ideas. Break them up into groups and

assign each group a topic. Allow the groups to teach their topic to the rest of the class. Topics: ethnic cleansing, Geneva talks, Lord Owen, Division of Bosnia, and Republic Day.

February 15—June 1, Pages 24-53

Vocabulary

civilians (24)	procession (24)	parliament (24)	barracks (24)
Muslim (29)	humanity (33)	revolting (35)	amputate (47)
dismembered (51)	hysterically (51)		

Discussion Questions

1. What is the significance of the blue flag and blue helmets? *(Answers will vary.)*

2. Do you agree that Zlata's parents should not allow her to watch the news? Why or why not? *(Answers will vary.)*

3. Who is Anne Frank? Why does Zlata mention Anne Frank in her diary? Why is it ironic that Zlata mentions Frank and her diary? *(Anne Frank was the author of a diary about World War II. Frank died in a concentration camp; Zlata also has a war diary; Answers will vary.)*

4. If you were Zlata's mother, would you have allowed her to go to the music concert? Why or why not? *(Answers will vary.)*

5. How do you think Zlata feels about the rumor of the bombing? *(She doesn't seem too concerned based on her writing.)*

6. What is the importance of the young girl's dying words, "Is this Sarajevo?" *(It emphasizes the differences between the normal circumstances in Sarajevo and the new ones.)*

7. What else could the families have done other than sending their children to another place? *(Answers will vary.)*

8. What image do you see when you are told that there are not enough buses and trains to hold all the people who wish to leave Sarajevo? *(Answers will vary.)*

9. Zlata writes that you have to be brave in order to stay behind with those you love. What is your definition of bravery? *(Answers will vary.)*

10. Why is it so tragic that an innocent little girl died? *(She had nothing to do with the war, and yet she was killed.)*

11. How does Zlata decide to change her writings? *(She is going to write about the war rather than herself.)*

12. What is Zlata trying to say when she mentions that she feels as if no one will survive? *(Answers will vary.)*

13. What would happen to your life if you were forced to stay indoors and away from the windows? *(Answers will vary.)*

14. **Prediction:** Is Zlata correct when she assumes that things will get better, or is she correct when she assumes that no one will survive? *(Answers will vary.)*

Supplementary Activities

1. Personal Interpretation: Have students write their opinion of Zlata's statement,"The people must be the ones to win, not the war, because war has nothing to do with humanity. War is something inhuman"(page 33).

2. Research: Ask the students to research Sarajevo's customs, religion, and holidays. Encourage them to share their information with their peers.

3. Creative Thinking: Ask the students to design a "safe house." Tell them to include the dimensions of the building and the necessary materials for building. Have them explain their reasoning. Encourage them to build a model. Ask them to construct a list of all the items that would need to be placed in the "safe house" in order to sustain life. Only allow them three frivolous items. Each item's importance must be explained.

June 5—September 21, Pages 54-83

Vocabulary

barrage (56)	servile (59)	humiliating (59)	liberated (66)
intervention (66)	pedigree (68)	sovereign (70)	hernia (74)

Discussion Questions

1. Zlata seems surprised that along with the war they are now running out of food. What other conditions are created due to war? *(Answers will vary.)*

2. Do you agree with Zlata's parents' decision to not tell her about the politics of the whole situation? Why or why not? *(Answers will vary.)*

3. Zlata pities the murderers for being so stupid. If you were in her position would you be able to pity them as well? Why or why not? *(Answers will vary.)*

4. Zlata talks about losing her childhood to the war. What effect might this have on her adulthood? *(Numerous possible answers.)*

5. We talk about fear in our daily lives—simple fear. Have you ever truly been afraid like Zlata is every time her mother tries to cross the bridge? Does her story change your idea of fear? *(Answers will vary.)*

6. Zlata mentions over and over that her life is her neighborhood—no longer her family. Who truly is your family, those to whom you are related or those who see you through tough times? *(Answers will vary.)*

7. Why is it that life is so complicated and almost impossible for Zlata and the others without water and electricity? People lived for hundreds of years without those luxuries; why is it difficult now? *(Answers will vary.)*

8. What does Zlata mean when she writes, "If only the war would stop, the wounds would heal"? *(Answers will vary.)*

9. Explain in your own words what it must have felt like for Zlata to be able to go out on her own to see her grandparents. *(Answers will vary.)*

10. What luxuries do you have in your life that you take for granted? What would you do if they were suddenly no longer accessible? *(Answers will vary.)*

11. Is it possible that you could ever end up in Zlata's situation? Why or why not? Did Zlata ever dream that she would find herself growing up in a war? *(Answers will vary.)*

12. Why is it that the kitten has helped to make Zlata's life more bearable? How can a small animal possibly make a terrible situation better? *(She was able to focus her energy on taking care of the kitten rather than worrying about herself.)*

13. Look at the picture of Zlata at her desk (after page 76). Is this how you imagined her life? How is it different from your visions? *(Answers will vary.)*

14. Is death regarded in the same way during war times as it is under normal situations? *(Answers will vary.)*

15. **Prediction:** Will the kitten and time with her friends be enough to distract Zlata from the war around her? *(Answers will vary.)*

Supplementary Activities

1. Character Analysis: Have students complete the Character Webs (pages 7-9 of this guide). Then ask the students to describe Zlata to the best of their ability. Ask them to explain what she might be like if she were a student in your class. Ask them to consider how she has changed due to the war.

2. Creative Thinking: Ask the students to pretend that they are in Zlata's situation. How might war change the way their family celebrates birthdays, holidays, or other special occasions?

3. Guest Speaker: Invite a guest speaker to talk to the class about living through a war. The students can prepare questions to ask the speaker. Discuss the responses, and as a class, determine if Zlata's life is similar to the information given by the guest speaker.

September 28—January 15, Pages 84-115

Vocabulary

convoy (84)	negotiating (85)	idiocy (95)	philosophizing (97)
condemned (98)	Adventist (111)		

Discussion Questions

1. If everyone is leaving, why isn't Zlata's family trying to escape? *(Perhaps they think things will start to get better.)*

2. Zlata expresses some anger toward the "kids." Do you think they are considering the people in their negotiations? How do politicians operate? Why do the people seem to feel left behind by those who are supposed to stand up for them? *(They seem to be in a battle of wits, and they do not seem too concerned about the well being of those who are in their care.)*

3. How does Zlata feel about Mimmy being published? How would you feel to have your journal published? Why? Does the knowledge that Mimmy will be published change your idea of what a journal is? Why or why not? *(Zlata is excited to have her diary published; Answers will vary.)*

4. What would you do if you were in Zlata's position? Would you leave with your mother and leave your father and grandparents behind? Why or why not? *(Answers will vary.)*

5. Do you agree with Zlata's opinion that the "young" could do politics better? *(Answers will vary.)*

6. How would you feel if you were told that you could not use the trees in your backyard for wood unless you purchased them from someone else? *(Answers will vary.)*

7. How is Zlata's twelfth birthday different from her eleventh? *(She receives more extravagant gifts for her eleventh birthday; for her twelfth she receives less, under the stressful circumstances.)*

8. What would happen if you found yourself in Braco's situation with his friend? What would you have done? Would you have behaved differently? *(Answers will vary.)*

9. Zlata writes that Mikica often forgets that all of the toys and belongings are gone. What would it be like to one day realize that you no longer have anything? What would you miss the most? Why? *(Answers will vary.)*

10. Do you think Zlata should have elbowed all of her friends in order to get some sweets at the Christmas party? What would you have done? *(Answers will vary.)*

11. What does Zlata mean when she writes that Mommy and Daddy look away from their books? *(They are probably thinking of the horrible situation in which they are living.)*

12. If you were in Zlata's situation, would you be excited to go to school? Why or why not? *(Answers will vary.)*

13. How is Sarajevo changing since the first few months of the war? *(The shooting doesn't seem to come as frequently.)*

14. If this war had happened in your neighborhood, how would it be different than it is in Zlata's hometown? *(Answers will vary.)*

Supplementary Activities

1. Literary Analysis: Zlata writes, "War has crossed out the day and replaced it with horror, and now horrors are unfolding instead of days" (page 96). Ask students to analyze this sentence. What literary methods does Zlata use? What is she referring to?

2. Service Project: Zlata is able to benefit from the help of many wonderful organizations, one of them being UNICEF. Encourage the students to come up with some type of service project that will help the community. Ask them to plan the project and follow through with it as a class or individually.

3. Math: Maja and Bojana live in a large house that measures 700 meters. Ask the students to determine how big that is in feet. Then compare that answer to a measurement of the schoolroom. Discuss the differences in the metric system. Ask the students if they think everyone should use the same type of measurement. Why or why not? What are the advantages or disadvantages? Discuss the other lessons Zlata learned from her math teacher such as arithmetic mean, ratios, and percentages.

January 24—May 20, Pages 116-141

Vocabulary

priority (116)	kilt (116)	cardigan (116)	marzipan (117)
refugees (122)	invalids (124)	radiation (126)	fortified (133)

Discussion Questions

1. Why does the small amount of electricity the family now has make Zlata happy when she is missing so many other things in life? *(They are happy with anything they can get to make life just a little more bearable.)*

2. Is it unusual that Zlata has become used to the war? What have you had to deal with in your life that originally you thought was unbearable? *(Answers will vary.)*

3. Zlata mentions the injured who have survived. Is it always a blessing to survive, or is it a misfortune? Explain your answers fully. Give specific examples. *(Answers will vary.)*

4. Why would the death of Cicko have such an impact on the family? Would it have affected them differently if it had occurred during peacetime? *(He was able to cheer them up with his song; he helped them to stay focused on hope. He was their tie to reality. Any other time it probably wouldn't have been so hard; however, it was now one more thing that the war had taken from them.)*

5. Reread Zlata's entry on April 17, 1993. Why is she so upset? What emotions do you think she is trying to convey? Is there anything else Zlata could do to make her situation more bearable? *(She is sick and tired of the war; she sees no end to it. She is at the point where she would rather die than to continue living under these conditions. Answers will vary.)*

6. If Zlata were to receive back all the items that she has lost during the war, do you think that would make her happy? *(Answers will vary.)*

7. If your community were in Zlata's situation, what would you do to help out your neighbors? Do you think that members of your community would help each other survive in the same manner? Do you help each other out even now? Why or why not? *(Answers will vary.)*

8. Zlata mentions the fear that surrounds them every day. Is she afraid of death or the unknown? Would her life have been better if she knew that this war was approaching? Would you want to know the future, even if you could not change it? Why or why not? *(Answers will vary.)*

9. What have the "kids" decided to do about dividing the town? Is this going to make the situation better or worse? Why or why not? *(Separating people always creates problems, especially if you are separating them based on race, religion, or culture.)*

10. What does Zlata mean when she says, "Politics don't ask ordinary people, only their own people"? *(The people who are being affected by this war are never considered in the decision-making process.)*

11. What happens when a mouse is in Zlata's house? Why does her mother worry? *(Zlata's mother is afraid of the mouse and worries about what it will eat or ruin. Zlata and her family think up ways to get rid of the mouse; Answers will vary.)*

12. Why is it such a horrible thought to Zlata that items are being sold for foreign money? *(They are things that should have belonged to the people of Sarajevo, and they are being sold for some other country's money. It seems as if some of the people have decided to accept the situation.)*

13. If you were in Nedo's shoes, would you return to Sarajevo? What would you do? Why? *(Answers will vary.)*

14. What do you learn about Daddy knowing that he doesn't think that Nedo will return? How is he different from Zlata? *(He thinks that Nedo should take advantage of the opportunity to escape Sarajevo. Zlata is more optimistic; she thinks he will return.)*

15. Look at the picture before page 141. Zlata is concerned about the impact that the war is having on her parents. What do you learn about Zlata, knowing that she is so worried about the well-being of her parents? *(She is compassionate and is concerned about others besides herself.)*

16. What would it be like to watch your parents become frail? *(Answers will vary.)*

17. **Prediction:** Is Nedo going to return to Sarajevo? *(Answers will vary.)*

Supplementary Activities

1. Discussion: Have the students consider and discuss the following questions and ideas. Is money the solution to all problems? When does money no longer matter? Consider Zlata's family's situation. Did they have money before the war? How has it helped them during the war? Are they treated differently? Do you think they care about the money now?

2. Critical Thinking: Zlata mentions that they are thinking of reopening the schools. However, the schools in her town have been destroyed or used for something else. Ask the students to think about their own town. If they were in Zlata's situation, what would the buildings in their area be used for? Tell them to consider the resources of each building and explain the rationale behind their answers. Ask them to draw a model of what their community or neighborhood might look like during a war.

3. Creative Thinking: Ask the students to pretend that Zlata will be coming to stay with their family for a week. What would they do to help her feel welcome? What questions would they have for her? How do they think she will feel about their lives? Ask the students to share their ideas with the class.

May 25—August 26, Pages 142-168

Vocabulary

inventive (159)   optimistic (165)   demilitarization (165)   suppressing (168)

Discussion Questions

1. What is Zlata's outlook on the war? *(She thinks she is going to die and even briefly contemplates killing herself. She doesn't see a happy end to the situation anymore.)*

2. Why do you think that Nedo has decided to run away? Does it have anything to do with his prior trip? *(Answers will vary.)*

3. What would happen if Nedo had offered to take Zlata with him? Would her parents have allowed her to go? Would she have gone? *(Answers will vary.)*

4. Why are Zlata's letters such a help to her in this sad time? *(They allow her to feel close to her friends.)*

5. One of the letters tells Zlata that good things happen to good people. Do you believe this idea? How do you explain war, death, hunger, and other bad things? *(Answers will vary.)*

6. If journalists are able to photograph and interview Zlata, why do you think they can't help the people of Sarajevo get out of a terrible situation? *(Answers will vary.)*

7. If you were Zlata, would you want to be compared to Anne Frank? Why or why not? What was Anne Frank's fate? *(Answers will vary; she died.)*

8. Zlata is afraid to hope for some type of agreement in Geneva because every time she expects something it doesn't happen. Do you agree with Zlata's philosophy? Why or why not? *(Answers will vary.)*

9. Mommy and Daddy often tell Zlata that "after the clouds comes the sun." Do you think they still believe that, or are they just trying to lift Zlata's spirits? *(Answers will vary.)*

10. Why does Zlata say that the "kids" really are just like children? *(They are playing with peoples' lives as if they are toys; they are setting up boundaries and not considering anyone but themselves.)*

11. Why do you suppose people are not getting any mail? *(Answers will vary.)*

12. Why would it be necessary to imitate ordinary life in order to make it bearable? *(If they pretend as if nothing is wrong, then perhaps they can find happiness for a short time.)*

13. What does Zlata mean when she writes, "We're learning to steel ourselves, this war is teaching us, and we're slowly suppressing everything that hurts us"? *(They are becoming stronger. Nothing that happens can affect them anymore. They expect the worst and are therefore prepared for it.)*

14. What do you do when times are difficult? Do you close yourself up so that you do not feel pain? Why or why not? *(Answers will vary.)*

15. **Prediction:** What is Zlata going to be like once this is all over? How would her personality change after such an ordeal? *(Answers will vary.)*

Supplementary Activities

1. Character Analysis: Ask the students to reread Zlata's entry on June 1, 1993. How is this entry different from most of the others? What would cause Zlata's mood to change so suddenly? Ask the students to consider how they might change under unusual circumstances.

2. Research: Ask the students to research the Muslim religious holidays Bairam and Kurban-Bairam. They should find out how and when these holidays started and what traditions surround them.

3. Metaphors: In Zlata's message read at the promotion she uses a metaphor to describe her life. She talks of lovely shores and a forced swimmer. Have students create a metaphor for Zlata's life and one for their own life.

August 27—Epilogue, Pages 169-197

Vocabulary

lodgers (169)	demolished (170)	enriched (170)	trove (171)
deteriorating (173)	obligations (173)	archive (175)	truces (177)
rationed (179)	illuminates (197)		

Discussion Questions

1. Why is it that everyone is leaving Sarajevo except Zlata and her family? Why do they decide to stay? *(Answers will vary.)*

2. What is the result of the "kids' little games," according to Zlata? *(Zlata says that 15,000 are dead in Sarajevo, 3,000 of them children, and 50,000 are permanent invalids.)*

3. Do you agree with Zlata that it is worse to lose mail delivery than water and electricity? Why? *(Answers will vary.)*

4. In your own words, can you describe what it would be like to look out of the windows and see so many people in wheelchairs and on crutches due to the war? Imagine knowing that there are not any places to bury the dead. How would you feel? *(Answers will vary.)*

5. Why does Daddy call their food "German" food? *(All of the food was bought with Duetsch Marks.)*

6. Zlata often wonders if they are alone in their situation. She doesn't think that anyone else thinks about them. Is she correct? Do you ever think of all the people who live in horrible conditions? Do you wonder what you can do to help them? Is Zlata really alone? *(Answers will vary.)*

7. What do you think kept the personnel carrier from coming to get Zlata and her family on December 8,1993? *(Answers will vary.)*

8. Why is it hard for Zlata to leave Sarajevo when she had been wishing to leave for nearly two years? *(She had to leave so many loved ones behind that she would probably never see again.)*

9. How would you feel if you had to leave everyone behind except for your mother and father? What if you were leaving them behind in horrible conditions like those in Sarajevo? *(Answers will vary.)*

10. How would you explain Zlata's elation at seeing the lights of Paris? *(She is thrilled to see evidence of electricity.)*

11. Why does Zlata mention that until some of the lights of Paris shine on Sarajevo they will not completely be her lights? *(She cannot fully enjoy them knowing that her loved ones in Sarajevo are still in the dark.)*

12. How could you convince Zlata to enjoy her new freedom and luxuries? *(Answers will vary.)*

13. Is there anything more Zlata could have done to help her friends in Sarajevo? Do you think she should have felt guilty about leaving? *(Answers will vary.)*

14. Have you ever had to move? How did you feel about leaving behind all of your friends? Can you relate to Zlata? *(Answers will vary.)*

15. **Prediction:** Imagine what Zlata's life is like now. How is it different? How has she changed? *(Answers will vary.)*

Supplementary Activities

1. Math: Ask the students to total up the number of people who have been killed or injured in the war in Sarajevo. Find a state or country that the students can relate to that is the same size as Sarajevo. Further, students can compare the fatality numbers from other wars to the numbers Zlata has given us.

2. Research: Ask the students to find out about other countries where people are living like Zlata. Ask them to consider how we can all live so differently in the same world.

3. Role-Playing: Have the class pretend that they have a brief opportunity to describe conditions in Sarajevo as Zlata would at a press conference. They should write a short speech expressing their opinions on the situation and a unique point of view on what it is like to live in the midst of war.

Post-reading Discussion Questions

1. Do you agree with Zlata's family's decision to finally leave Sarajevo?

2. What might Zlata's life be like today? How do you imagine the war changed her?

3. What did you learn about war from reading Zlata's account?

4. What else could Zlata's family have done to make the situation more bearable?

5. How would you go about writing a treaty to solve the problem in Sarajevo?

6. Who is your favorite character in the story? Why?

7. Do you think Zlata is stronger for having lived through the war, or is she worse off for having witnessed such atrocities?

8. Zlata knows early on that her diary will be published. What evidence do you find of this? Do you think it may have influenced her writing? How?

9. How can we use Zlata's retelling of the war to help us in our daily lives?

10. What is the main idea or theme of the story?

11. If Zlata had to reduce her book down to one page, what do you think she would put on that page? Why?

12. How does reading a personal diary account of a war differ from reading a newspaper account or a historical text, or watching a television report?

13. How do you think Zlata's family obtains permission to leave Sarajevo when so many others cannot?

Post-reading Extension Activities

1. How does Zlata change in the course of her story? Write a compare/contrast paper showing Zlata before the war and Zlata after the war.

2. Zlata mentions that she has been compared to Anne Frank. Read *The Diary of Anne Frank*. Discuss as a class the similarities and differences between the two books.

3. Create either a crossword puzzle or a word search using the vocabulary words.

4. Do some research to find out what Sarajevo is like today. Report your findings to the class.

5. Pretend that you are Zlata. Write a monologue that you could perform for the class describing your situation.

6. Write a letter to Zlata. Ask her all of the questions that were unanswered by the story. Mention specific passages and details from the text. Share your letters with the class.

7. Illustrate one of the scenes from the novel. Try to work closely with the information given to describe the area.

8. Create a current events group. Bring a current event to school each day to discuss. Mark the location mentioned in the article on a map. If children are involved, talk about what they must be dealing with in each situation.

9. Make a mobile that expresses Zlata's personality.

10. Personalize the journal you started while reading *Zlata's Diary* with drawings, stickers, etc. Observe the picture opposite page 140 to see an example of Zlata's personalized journal.

11. Complete the Story Map on page 10 of this guide. Fill in detailed information about the book and include page numbers to support your evidence.

Assessment for *Zlata's Diary*

Assessment is an ongoing process. The following eleven items can be completed during the novel study. Once finished, the student and teacher will check the work. Points may be added to indicate the level of understanding.

Name ____ Date _______________________

Student   **Teacher**

______   ______   1. Create a collage that represents war and peace. Use magazine pictures, words, original drawings, etc. Be creative.

______   ______   2. Invent a board game about Zlata's life. Include all necessary parts.

______   ______   3. Create a 30-second commercial for peace.

______   ______   4. Write a poem about war based on what you know. Write it from Zlata's experience or based on other accounts you have read.

______   ______   5. Build a model of Zlata's living conditions during the war. Use the book to help with your accuracy.

______   ______   6. Write a persuasive speech or letter asking for Zlata's grandparents to be allowed to leave Sarajevo.

______   ______   7. Create a talk show in which you are able to interview Zlata and other refugees.

______   ______   8. Take a survey in your school; find out how many people are aware of the problems in Sarajevo and other countries. What can you do to help educate them?

______   ______   9. Incorporate current events into the morning announcements at your school for one week. Be creative.

______   ______   10. Write a monologue stating your own personal experience with hardship or loss.

______   ______   11. Write a short skit based on the ending of *Zlata's Diary*. Who would you use to play the main characters? What major theme or message would you try to give to the audience?

Notes